First Facts®

U.S. Military Forces

THE UNITED STATES MARINES

by Michael Green

CAPSTONE PRESS
a capstone imprint

First Facts are published by Capstone Press.
1710 Roe Crest Drive, North Mankato, Minnesota 56003
www.capstonepub.com

Library of Congress Cataloging-in-Publication Data
Green, Michael, 1952–
    The United States Marines / by Michael Green.
    p. cm.—(First facts)
    Audience: Grades K-3.
    Includes bibliographical references and index.
    Summary: "Provides information on the training, missions, and equipment used by the
United States Marines"—Provided by publisher.
    ISBN 978-1-4765-0072-0 (library binding)
    ISBN 978-1-4765-1586-1 (eBook PDF)
1. United States. Marine Corps—Juvenile literature. 2. Marines—United States—Juvenile
literature. I. Title.
VE23.G75 2013
359.9'60973—dc23   2012033248

Editorial Credits
Aaron Sautter, editor; Ashlee Suker, designer; Eric Manske, production specialist

Photo Credits
Painting by V. Zveg courtesy of the U.S. Navy Art Collection, Washington, D.C., 6; U.S. Marine Corps photo,
12, Cpl. Brian J. Slaght, 18, Cpl. Gabriela Garcia, 1, Gunnery Sgt. Bryce Piper, 17, Lance Cpl. Ali Azimi, cover,
Lance Cpl. Benjamin Crilly, 21, Lance Cpl. Emmanuel Ramos, 15, Sgt. Brandon Saunders, 10, Sgt. Eric D.
Warren, 20, Sgt. Ezekiel R. Kitandwe, 5, Sgt. Ricardo A. Gomez, 9, Sgt. Whitney N. Frasier, 13; U.S. Navy
Photo by MC2 Michael Russell, 19

Artistic Effects
Shutterstock: Kirsty Pargeter, Redshinestudio, Vilmos Varga

5203 4377
7/13

Printed in the United States of America in North Mankato, Minnesota.
092012   006933CGS13

TABLE OF CONTENTS

FIRST TO FIGHT

Loud gunfire fills the air as U.S. Marines **raid** an enemy camp. They search the buildings and quickly capture an enemy leader. The Marines take him back to their ship. They then prepare for their next **mission**. The U.S. Marines are always ready for action.

raid—a sudden, surprise attack on a place
mission—a military task

FACT

A Marine battle unit includes 2,200 troops and more than 150 military vehicles.

The Continental Congress created the Marines on November 10, 1775. At first the Marines were part of the U.S. Navy. In 1798 Congress created a separate U.S. Marine Corps. It worked closely with the U.S. Navy and still does today.

The Marines protect the United States and help people in need. They fight enemies on land, air, and sea.

FACT

Marines often bring food, water, and supplies to help countries suffering from natural disasters.

CHAPTER TWO

MIGHTY MARINES

The U.S. Marine Corps is one of the strongest military forces in the world. More than 200,000 active Marines serve their country. Nearly 40,000 **reserves** also stand ready to fight. The Marines quickly respond to threats against the United States. They are often the first troops called to battle.

reserves—troops that stay ready for active duty but are not full-time soldiers

Most people in the Marines are **enlisted** men and women. Every Marine is trained to fight. But these soldiers do many other jobs. Some work with electronics or computers. Others work on vehicles and planes. Marines work to keep their units ready for action.

Marine officers take command during missions. They lead troops into battle.

CHAPTER THREE

BECOMING A MARINE

Marine **recruits** go through 12 weeks of basic training. They wake up before dawn every day. They run many miles and go through obstacle courses. They also train to become experts with weapons.

After basic training recruits learn
the skills needed for their Marine jobs.
Marines can work as engineers, combat
specialists, and do many other jobs.

recruit—a new member of the armed forces

The top Marines often attend Officer Candidate School. There they learn how to command troops in battle.

People with college degrees can take a 10-week Officer Candidate Course. College students can go to Platoon Leaders Class. These programs teach people the leadership skills needed to become officers.

CHAPTER FOUR

EQUIPPED TO FIGHT

The U.S. Marines use some of the world's best military equipment. Marines carry advanced machine guns, rifles, and other small weapons. They also use heavy weapons such as howitzers and mortars.

FACT

Marines also use rockets and missiles such as the FGM-148 Javelin Anti-tank Missile.

Marines use high-tech gear.
Night-vision scopes help them fight
enemies in the dark. **Laser** systems
help Marines easily hit their targets.

laser—a narrow, intense beam of light

AMPHIBIOUS ASSAULT VEHICLE

Amphibious Assault Vehicles (AAVs) carry Marines and gear from ships to land. Powerful Abrams tanks help Marines fight enemies on land.

amphibious—able to work on land or water

A/V-8B Harriers and Super Cobra helicopters provide great firepower in battle. Super Stallion helicopters and Hercules planes carry troops and heavy cargo.

SUPER COBRA

FACT

The EA-6B Prowler fighter plane can find, jam, and destroy enemy radar.

CHAPTER FIVE

READY FOR BATTLE

The Marines use the best equipment. Assault Breacher Vehicles clear land **mines** off roads. The RQ-7B Shadow is an unmanned aircraft. It helps find enemy locations from a safe position.

RQ-7B SHADOW

mine—an explosive device; land mines are buried underground

ASSAULT BREACHER VEHICLE

Marine troops and vehicles can be
sent into battle quickly. U.S. Marines are
always ready to fight for their country.

GLOSSARY

amphibious (am-FI-bee-uhs)—able to work on land or water

enlist (in-LIST)—to voluntarily join a branch of the military

laser (LAY-zur)—a narrow, intense beam of light

mine (MINE)—an explosive device; land mines are buried underground

missile (MISS-uhl)—an explosive weapon that can travel long distances

mission (MISH-uhn)—a military task

obstacle course (OB-stuh-kuhl KORSS)—a series of barriers that Marines must jump over, climb, or crawl through

radar (RAY-dar)—a device that uses radio waves to track the location of objects

raid (RAYD)—a sudden, surprise attack on a place

recruit (ri-KROOT)—a new member of the armed forces

reserves (ri-ZURVZ)—troops that stay ready for active duty but are not full-time soldiers

READ MORE

David, Jack. *United States Marine Corps.* Armed Forces. Minneapolis: Bellwether Media, 2008.

Goldish, Meish. *Marine Corps: Civilian to Marine.* Becoming a Soldier. New York: Bearport Pub., 2011.

Shank, Carol. *U.S. Military Assault Vehicles.* U.S. Military Technology. North Mankato, Minn.: Capstone Press, 2013.

INTERNET SITES

FactHound offers a safe, fun way to find Internet sites related to this book. All of the sites on FactHound have been researched by our staff.

Here's all you do:

Visit *www.facthound.com*

Type in this code: 9781476500720

Super-cool stuff! Check out projects, games and lots more at **www.capstonekids.com**

INDEX